Swirling Eddies

The beginning scribbles

Keziah K Glidden

BALBOA.PRESS

A DIVISION OF HAY HOUSE

Balboa Press books may be ordered through booksellers or by contacting:

Balboa Press
A Division of Hay House
1663 Liberty Drive
Bloomington, IN 47403
www.balboapress.com
844-682-1282

Because of the dynamic nature of the Internet, any web addresses or
links contained in this book may have changed since publication and
may no longer be valid. The views expressed in this work are solely those
of the author and do not necessarily reflect the views of the publisher,
and the publisher hereby disclaims any responsibility for them.

The author of this book does not dispense medical advice or prescribe the use
of any technique as a form of treatment for physical, emotional, or medical
problems without the advice of a physician, either directly or indirectly. The
intent of the author is only to offer information of a general nature to help
you in your quest for emotional and spiritual well-being. In the event you use
any of the information in this book for yourself, which is your constitutional
right, the author and the publisher assume no responsibility for your actions.

Print information available on the last page.

ISBN: 978-1-9822-5575-6 (sc)
ISBN: 978-1-9822-5577-0 (hc)
ISBN: 978-1-9822-5576-3 (e)

Library of Congress Control Number: 2020918910

Balboa Press rev. date: 10/02/2020

Contents

It truly
Was soft
Light, that met
My eyes
With a kiss
"Good Morning"
Said the sun

I wake when you wake

Bring a dream
To the table
Let me gulp it down
Let it sting and sizzle
As I down another round.

One shot

How do you feel?

Look at the flowers
Be still
They are not named
I am,_
Remains a void
Of stillness
The petals are airy
And light
No longer do you look
To name
But look
To feel

To not lose the magic

Purple smears
On circumference of blue.
Petals, speckled with dotted age.
Humble heads,
Greet the greatest God,
And release their sweet
Invisible perfume.
"I long to be admired."
There is nothing
Happened, now or before.
Purple smears
that only exist now.

Existing

O Lord,
What is it?
Love.
O dear,
You feel.
Feelings are proof enough.
To only love when it is lost.
That is regret.
Love the sounds, smells, sights.
Love from the unknown.

O Lord

Sunset
A deep shovel
Full of red dirt
Buries
Another day
Spreading across
Healing the things
That lay beneath

Only those meant to be
Will dig themselves out
To find the
Sunrise

To rise

A dirt road and yellow roses
Poking their heads
Out from hiding
One red rose
Stands in the middle.
But it's too late
To grab it
Hold it
Smell it
Only yellow roses stretch on
Hiding their red roots.

Hiding red roots

Linger for this moment
Hold still
Time
Please hold still
Awhile longer
If only I could hold you here
In my mind
I'd *never* look away.
The upturned *curve*
Under your eyes.
Hold us here
A little while longer
Your *sweet like honey*
Smile.
Your *blue* golden
Eyes.
You heart, and very
Soul,
Pouring out into this world.
We *do not* deserve your sweet face.
This turning ball of fires
Does not deserve your
Spirit
Of *daisies.*
Your spirit of *gentle* streams
...And oh, not so gentle
Rivers
The rushing
Spiraling
Rivers
That envelope each new ground they touch
Giving life,
Quenching fires,
And only living for the moment to rush on
And find the thirsting grounds.
Ah...
Stop *here.*
Linger,
On these moments that move away too fast.
Let's slip under the eddies that pull us down,
And stay awhile longer.

8.11.20 *Eddies*

You see with
Much
More than the eyes

You feel,
Touch,
Much
More than I touch

Hearts
Souls
Souls
Hearts

You are
Much
More
Than a human

Alien depths

Translucent light
Kisses my crown
And seeps down to my collarbones.
Met from below
A turning awakeness
Plants in my feet,
And swims up
Filling and filling
Till light and light touch,
Caressing in the middle
Of my chest.
They cradle each other,
And my body is home
To beautiful energies.

Light energies

I could write forever about
How much I care for your laugh.

Only so many songs I could listen to,
Whistles of waking robins at sunrise,
Rush of waterfalls in paradise,
Pushing and pulling of the sea on sandy beaches,
Snowstorms with promises of inconvenience,
Fires crackling in warm summer night,
Rain hitting rooftops at midnight.

Only your laugh
Will wrap me up
Wash over me
and snuggle next to my heart

Only your laugh
Will entrance me
For the rest of my life.

Entrancing

Dark Sky
Sprinkled with fireflies
Shooting stars cross the night above
It's dying breath
"Make a wish" you say
A wish?
What would I wish of?
Unseen futures? Possibilities?
So a wish
I said to you.
a wish of promise and renewal
To me.
I wished for many more dying breaths to come.

Many more

We talked for hours together.
Not alone in each old mind
But of things that made us talk louder
And explained thoughts beyond the simple.
The pauses fit in nicely.
I watched you smile wider
The fire in your eyes.
Realizing the truth.
We fit.
A green communication
For outsiders looking in.
When I held your hand,
they saw your baggage fade to white.

A holy dialogue

Drum your hands on the belly of the earth
I can hear your sound

It thumps to my heart
And my heart cannot help
But sing

Louder, louder

Still I hear
Chorus of drums
Beating our path
Singing our song

We quiet for nothing
Quiet for no one

I forever sing to the sound of your drum

Belly of the earth

So
I float on clouds that fall back to earth

A pillow and open sky
I lay down and close my eyes
To lift above the haze and fly
Through the tips of Pine trees
that reach high

Through only the tallest mountain.
Sweeping down and kissing its nose.
Then drifting to rest above the sea
And dipping in my toes

But
I float on clouds that must fall back to earth...
A journey I must awaken for.

Day dreams

Bend
Fold
Twist
Mold

Reach toes up to clouds
And hook onto the rains

Open up and pour through you
To water dry ground

Send shooting light
Out the top of your crown

Stretch your head to the sky.
Toes to the earth.
Arch your back
And
Sink
      Sink
           Sink
Onto the ground.
Your home.
Sink farther.

This is
Your cradling hammock.

Your cradling hammock

So I ask you…
Explain yourself
And you tell me
This
That
Here
There
But I stop you for the moment
In your rambling.
You are not *anything* you say you are
You cannot explain yourself away
For you are so much more
than what you tell me.

unexplainable

You are enveloping.
Your rhythms enrapture me.
Dipping cold feet
Cold feet
I didn't have them until
I dipped in
It stung.
Cold feet
I didn't have them
much longer it seemed.
All went numb below
The gentle ripples.

Sweet cold ice river

When I leave
My honeycomb home,
I waken my wings
And hope to find
Sweet nectar in places I land.
Find fields of flowers
And low breeze buzzing.

Take flight

I try to grasp them whole
These memories that loosen their grasp.

Once an experience
Becomes
Memory...
Heavy they seem.
Nothing is more tangible
Then the moment I'm in.

I let my fingers slip away from heavy ones.
Grasping those that fall into my hand
These lighter moments...

(In)*tangible*

Believe me, my heart
When I tell you it's fine to squeeze
And feel the uneasiness.
The uncertainty in making
A wrong decision
Believe me, I hear, *feel* you inside me.
Your patters do not go unnoticed
The soft thrum in the solitude
And rapid wings escaping
In times of evolving
I feel you squeezing me tight
In warning of a future
When the strings attach to another.
Believe me when I tell you
We must open to another
And I will place you *gently* in their hands

Trust me

If only you knew
The white sky above
When I see that smile.
A lily blossoms inside
White lilies.
Pure
White.
I could sit and stare for *hours.*
Time would fall away
Worlds would move on without us,
And I would be sitting
Staring at you smiling.
Just white skies above.

Innocence

These surface levels...
With shallow ponds beneath.
Hold nothing but stagnant waters.

Your deep oceans,
These *levels* you layer,
Go deep beyond the normal.
Your deep waters
Hold wonders that the world *wished* they could see.

Deeply feeling

To pour it into
Your very soul,
And saturate
The smallest holes.
This is it.
No more questions
To be asked.
To eat from one tree for the rest of eternity.

Faith

Below the waterline
Is easy to float away.
Hold nothing in
But air
Nothing to keep safe inside.
Float or sink to
No-thing
No moving
No sounds
Below the waterline
And above the clouds.
Stepping on no-thing air.

Sink to float

Breathing fire.
They said they breathed
Fire on the world
And
Millions lined up
To burn.

To feel

To each piece
The rhyme
No reason.
Each piece
Seen put together
As a family.
An unfinished puzzle
Neverending
To welcome all
That wander
To connect
And be family

My family

We are slipping
Down waterfalls
Falling in a falling
World.
Streams block out metal on metal
And
Sparkling waters
Cover over
The black oil
Spilling, slipping
Under stairwells
And soaking
Homes.
We are floating
At the bottom
Of waterfalls
Slipping
In and out of
This world.
Float on your back
And keep your head up
Dear one.

Peace among chaos

My Stories...

A story of a person who had *dreams*
Bigger than anyone had perceived
Compare them to the
Sun
Moon
Stars
But *vaster*
So unexplainable they reached *so high* they became the heavens
of stars
So high the angels shouted of their beauty
Dreams of *lives*
Dreams of *becoming*
Having. Doing. Being.
They twirled in the vastness of her mind
Longing to wrap around and intertwine
And certain ones did
They wound around tight
And *they grew*
A dream that grew so big
That *nothing* could stop the beautiful unfolding into reality.

My story

Bees
I saw them float
Up above the mint field.
They were going home.
Relocation.
To follow a queen
Who had tired of mint.

Bumble
Tumble

Mint Fields

I walked through an alley
Dark on a bright summer day.
Partial souls lined the streets sidewalks
Rolling up said sorrows
Into pieces of paper
And drowning reality
If only to dream.
To walk without knowing where.
To see without thinking.
And at that moment
I wished I sat and prayed.
But,
I shook hands,
And gave brown paper lunches
To the hands of partial souls.

Brown paper lunches

Once a strong woman took up a vessel
She sailed the bright sea,
and with it she wrestled

She sailed through the waves and fought the load roar
From the wind who knocked
Knocked
Knocked
At her door

The strong woman had fought for years.
Storms and downpours,
empty waves brought tears.

Her vessel was barren
The floorboards groaned
The sea held one person
All else were disowned

There was no child
No baby to hold
No spirit of the wind
No stories be told

She sailed out alone
With no one to guide
her
Looking for treasure
No one besides
her

One night
at sea, all was clear.
The God, she knew,
made it appear.

An island she saw in the distance ahead
To the top of the mountain, she dared tread
And she found the
baby bathed in dripping gold light.
Wrapped up in her arms,
nothing else felt right.

It did not matter the color, the size.
On top of that mountain laid her treasured prize.

With soft cooing, laughing and blubbering cries
She knew the voyage was worth seeing its eyes.

Down the mountain she went
Knowing time was well spent
"Be fulfilled for once" was all the sea meant

Sleeping in her arms
She climbed on board.
The sea held two people,
they both were Adored

By the sea and the winds and the world... unexplored
By two people.

Above the sails soared.

They drifted off into sunny nowhere
Another voyage--
now to be shared.

Wrapped up in her arms, she held a future
A squirmy, beautiful, happy creature.

Adoption

She walked into the room
Her chin was held up high

They asked her for a reason
And this she said was why

"It was my choice."

Her petals blew in slight breeze

Little roots held her down

"I came for me and women after
I came for the joys of little girl laughter"

She watched shifty eyes and clicking tongues
"You have too much" they say
And one by one they plucked her petals,
on the floor they lay.

There was no need to shout or cry
Her roots held deep below.

Then the room went dark and no light was found
Until morning rays came round
The sun broke through the silence,
She picked her petals off the ground

"Why did you come?"
Ravens cackled above

She raised her head up high

"I came for the women
- delicate but strong flowers-
To show that the sun, light and everything bright
Gives us untouchable powers."

Courageous

71

She sang for the old ears
A sound that brought tears
To the eyes of those
who saw many years

She sang of today
She sang of new ways
How to stay loyal
and not to betray

Not a song of tomorrow
Or all days to follow
She sang of today
and I asked to borrow...

Her *Wisdom*
Please, let me follow your drum
The song needs only
Your reminding hum

Hum me the song
As I add the word
Whistle a tune
as sweet as a bird
Don't leave now,
I want to be heard...

I wish for one moment
time would just *freeze*
Stay for the end of the song
like the trees

Who stand tall and wait
For whistles end late
In the deepness of night
Birdsongs dissipate.

See? The trees waited for the end
Won't you wait longer, dear friend?
I promise you broken branches i'll mend
If you only stay to the end.

We leave on different notes

Shambles of soft shattered
Sidewalk separates the streets.

She sees him standing solemn and sad
On the sideways sort of sidewalk

A spark of surprising spontaneous action

She saunders to him

"See the sidewalk" she said
"Looking sad in it's solitude."

"I say we sell everything.
Sell our stores and savings.
Fix the sad sidewalk that separates the streets."

She sank to the ground to start on the sidewalk
His self sank too

They slaved and suffered and much they sacrificed for the
sidewalk
And soon, the sidewalk began to shine.
After seven solid years it was no longer in shambles.
They saved the streets that it joined.

Figures of sacrifice

Belly ballooning
Empty with air
Filled up with nothing
"Pretend something's there"

Fill it with bark
Trash
Things you find off the street
Fill it with something
Anything?
"Mamma, there's nothing to eat."

The bear is my enemy
He lives deep inside
He's selfish and loud
Grumbling
Soon I can't hide

"Mamma i'm hungry"
Pappa's not here
"Mamma i'm starving"
Darkness draws near

Darkness pulls in
Folds over my eyes
My mamma's laying next to me
I can't hear her cries

I'm starving mamma

Tree branches
Folded around her

She assumed a position of
Defeat
And the earth came to defend

It sheltered and fed sweet fruits.
Its roots held water.

She stayed until her fingers
Intertwined
With the hands of trees.
And arms lifted her up

It held her closer and closer.

Until another soul fell to the ground.

And she sheltered,
Fed,
And watered.

Intertwining with the fingers of a fallen,
And one became many.

One became many

Dear deer on that
Dreary dirt hill

Hear how heaven
Hails rain on your head?

Sweet scents waft swiftly
Down streams

Rain rises
Flowers to reign

Behold beloved
bellowing bear

Careful to catch catfish
Dropping from clouds

Drip drop they flop
In deep dark ponds

Protected by perfect
Picturesque lily pads

Hello heroic
Heavenly horses

Together you tread
Till tomorrows trumpets trill

Animals arrive in amiable arrangements

Drinking together from the drip dropping pond.

Dear deer

Where do you stand
In green and gray smoke?
Burning
Cigs and houses
Together they burn to the ground.

It's black or white.

Stoic faces staring down
Gray
Green
Smoke
clouding the middle.
No standing tall in the middle.

Big breath
Blow
the house down.
To see where they stand
And lay

No more smoke
Just survival

Our survival

She grabbed
her paint

On the floor, the canvas lay
Smearing through the wet
She slashed with bristled daggers
Before the paint had set

Whites and blacks,
One color in between.
The simple gray was holding on
To anything it seemed.

Crumble and
Flakes
The pictures
She made
Lying
In shambles
On the floor

Dad demanded
"Pick up the pieces!"
Mom left,
And offered her reasons

No masterpiece was left.
Nothing to admire.
She tore the canvas down the middle
And threw away her pile

Broken masterpiece

We passed a memory
Like floating through
-in and out-
Of a cloudy dream
I reimagined the moment,
Sitting on the grass
And talking about you
And it all
Tumbled in and fell away
As we rode on

Bike ride

Softly, the first drop falls from the sky. A lone tear and the rest tumble behind.
I reach my hands up to grab them,
Capture them in my hands. They hit the dirt and leave muddy feet.
Freely dancing through the sky and planting each drop on the earth.
The beats move my body,
Inviting me to dance along.
So I stare open mouthed up at gray clouds and sway to the uniformity surrounding me.
Swing
Spin
They travel down my skin
and I bathe in new waters.
This stopped moment in time,
And I thank the earth
For bringing happiness.
-Tears rip open the sky then fall to cover us all-
I thank the earth for softening the ground below
And the hard edges within.

7.24.20

A pavement
Lined with pine trees
And I'm a child again
Walking down a lane of memories
A single tree
I swing across
I climbed it
Climbed higher than the roof
And sat above the world.

Yes she saw herself,
A little girl,
And wanted her to know
These trees lined the path to the house.
Their gentle limbs guiding her home.

Memory lane

A brown barn splits
Across expansions
Of unnecessary,
Necessary growth.
And a brown barn
Hides among the friendly foliage
Hiding out
Waiting for the forgotten
To be remembered
To be cut down
To be forgotten.

Forgotten relics